FENWAY IN YOUR POCKET

The Red Sox Fan's Guide to Fenway Park

Kevin T. Dame

Published by Dame Publishing
Design by Christine Dame Yoshida
Illustrations by Ryoji Yoshida, Kevin Dame, and
Christine Dame Yoshida.

First Printing
Printed in the United States of America

This book may be ordered directly from the publisher by
sending a check or money order for $4.95 per book plus
$2.00 shipping and handling to: Baseball Direct,
Department B4, P.O. Box 41289, Providence, RI 02940.

This book is not endorsed by the Boston Red Sox or
Fenway Park.

Acknowledgements

To Christine and Ryoji, my grateful appreciation for all your patience and hard work.

My sincere thanks to the Boston Red Sox, Harry M. Stevens, and the MBTA for their assistance.

Thanks also to my family and my friends who have offered me so much support throughout this project.

And special thanks to the 1986 Red Sox, who sparked my incurable fascination with baseball.

Contents

Chapter Three: Play Ball!

Preface

What makes Boston different? Most of you will immediately respond "Our crazy drivers," and this is indeed a fine answer. But putting aside our reputation for absolute chaos on the roadways, the more accurate answer is: our sports. Contrary to our less intelligent counterparts in New York, Boston is the holy land for the avid sports fan. Nowhere in the country can one find our collection of tradition-steeped sports franchises combined with such a large and faithful population of sports fanatics. And among all of the sports landmarks in Boston, we have something truly special that no other sports fan has — Fenway Park.

This book is about Fenway Park, one of the last original baseball parks from baseball's early years. In an era of generic baseball stadiums, Fenway serves as a reminiscent reminder of the way baseball used to be. A night at Fenway is probably little different from one fifty years ago when Ted

Williams was terrorizing opposing American League pitchers.

This book is not about boring history or "who cares" trivia. It is a user's guide to Fenway, written for you, the Fenway parishioner, to help you get the most out of your experience at the game without the usual hassles. It will also help you leave with a few bucks left in your pocket. Whether it's a helpful tip on where to park your car, or a review of the "Fenway Beer rules," you'll be coached, step by step, throughout the entire Fenway experience.

I hope that this book finds a permanent home in your jacket pocket whenever you plan a trip to the park. For those of you who have never been to Fenway, shame on you! Fenway won't be around forever, and if you call yourself a sports fan (or even a New Englander, for that matter!) you owe it to yourself to make a trip to cheer on your Red Sox at least once.

As you join the two–million plus fans who enter Fenway this summer, take this book along with you and you'll be guaranteed a great time.

CHAPTER ONE

FENWAY BASICS

Fenway Oath

"Fenway Park is a shrine where people come for religious rites." – Former Red Sox pitcher Bill Lee

Before we begin, every Fenway visitor must learn the basic rule of fanhood — the Fenway oath:

> On my honor, I promise to cheer on
> my Red Sox, to devour Fenway franks and
> peanuts, to properly execute the "Fenwave,"
> and to soak in the fresh air, smells, sights,
> and sounds of Fenway, until I am truly at peace.

Wise sages have determined that if someday every fan at Fenway could simultaneously achieve this higher level of consciousness for one game, the "Curse of the Bambino," which has stolen many a championship from our grasp, might finally be lifted.

Fenway Park: History 101

In 1911, with baseball in its infancy, Red Sox owner John Taylor purchased land in Boston's Fenway section and built a new ball park for the team. Nicknamed "Fenway Park Grounds," it opened in 1912, replete with the latest in ballpark design. While its character and charm have been maintained over the years, there have been some facelifts — most notably the electronic centerfield scoreboard erected in 1976, the lights added in 1947, and the 600 Club (additional seats indoors) in 1988. This recent addition altered the strong wind currents which formerly traveled from home plate outwards. Many experts, especially over-the-hill power hitters, suspect that this has reduced the frequency of home runs hit at Fenway.

The 1912 version of Fenway possessed a steep embankment in front of the left field wall called Duffy's Cliff. The 10 ft. high cliff was named after Red Sox left fielder Duffy Lewis who was known for his defensive prowess around the hill. The cliff was removed in 1933. As the years progressed, Fenway's seating capacity fluctuated. It now stands at 33,871, although more can be squeezed in through the novel concept of "standing room only" sections. Fenway's largest crowd occurred on September 22, 1935, when over 47,000 fans attended a game against the arch rival Yankees. A paltry crowd of 409 cheered on the Red Sox against the Angels on September 29, 1965 representing Fenway's smallest crowd ever.

Home runs have always been a part of Fenway's history, starting in 1912 with a seventh inning blast over the wall by Hugh Bradley. Curiously, in the early years there were very few home runs hit by the Sox at home. In fact, in 1916 the Red Sox hit only one home run at Fenway. Three years later a new, livelier baseball was introduced, and the Red Sox, led by Babe Ruth's record 29 home runs, hit 33 out of the park.

Season Time Line

Let's get some perspective here before we go too far. The true baseball fan realizes that even though the season officially ends in October, in reality it continues on throughout the winter and into spring. Your time away from Fenway during the "off-season" is a time for you to reflect on the previous season, speculate on possible trades and free-agent acquisitions, and to mentally psyche yourself up for the next season. By March you should be experiencing serious withdrawal pains, and eagerly anticipating opening day at Fenway!

Take a look at the calendar and see why the season really lasts all year long.

Fenway Fan's Twelve-Month Planner

January
Winter ball in S. America

February
Players prep for spring training

March
Spring Training Games!

April
Opening Day!

May
Sox pull out in front!

June
College baseball draft

July
All-Star Game!

August
Listen to Sox games on beach

September
Pennant Fever!

October
Playoffs and Word Series

November
Debate trades w/friends

December
Winter Mtgs: new players for Xmas!

Fenway Fast-Facts

For those of you who are trapped in the fast-paced lifestyle of the 90s, you need the most important information boiled down to a simple, easy to read format that even a chimpanzee could understand. (For the people who typically read USA Today and only read the blurbs on the bottom left of the front page, these FAST-FACTS are for you!)

Fenway Park
4 Yawkey Way, Boston, MA 02215
(617) 267-1700

Home games: 81 games (April to October)
Game times: 1:05 pm (Day), 7:05 pm (Night)
TV Coverage: NESN, WSBK TV38
Radio Coverage: WRKO 680 AM

Additional Fast-Facts: To order the 1994 Red Sox Media Guide, send $8 to 4 Yawkey Way, Boston, MA 02215. To order the Official Red Sox Scorebook Magazine, send $3 to the same address.

8

CHAPTER TWO

PRE-GAME WARM-UPS

Selecting a Game

The art of selecting the perfect game is based upon five important factors. Whether it be for your family, the date you're trying to impress, or a business client, considering these five factors will help make your time at Fenway all the more enjoyable:

1. Weather and time of day
2. Time of season
3. The opponent
4. Pitching match-ups
5. Red Sox promotions.

Weather

The most important thing is to be comfortable! The prospects of shivering in the face of cold, gusting winds, squinting through your rain-soaked glasses, or passing out due to 90 degree temperatures can all be eliminated if you properly dress for the weather and time of day. In April, and again in September, you may need a winter jacket, a sweater, and possibly a hat, gloves, and even thermal underwear. Remember, you'll be sitting outside in one place for three hours. For those of you who think that drinking alcohol keeps you warm outside in cold weather (college students, pay attention) — you're wrong! The alcohol slows down your metabolism and opens up the pores in your skin. You could actually get hypothermia!

In the middle of the season, during Boston's warmest weather, shorts and T-shirts suffice during the day, while a wind-breaker is usually a good idea to have with you during night games. Certain areas of the park (especially the bleachers) are exposed to strong sunshine, so during the summer make sure to bring a supply of sunscreen or you may end up as red as the players' socks. Reserved Grandstand seats are mostly shielded from the rain, and during a rain delay you will be protected. However, if you are in an unprotected zone (bleachers), make sure you bring a small umbrella just in case. (See "Picking the Best Place to Sit" on page 25 for more information.) Even when rain is forecasted, a common occurrence in Boston summers, grab a wind breaker and umbrella and head to the ballpark — it's still worth going because many games are still played after only a short delay. You can get a better idea of the likelihood of a game being called off by calling the Red Sox at (617) 267–8661, or listening to WRKO 680 AM on the radio for the latest rain information.

Time of Season

The time of season strongly influences ticket availability, the size of crowds, and the general atmosphere inside the park. The first month of the season is an exciting time for fans (especially opening day), but seats are a bit easier to get due to the colder weather. During the dog days of summer (late July through August), games are often sold out, yet many fans lose a little interest and turn their attention to barbecues, trips to the beach, and members of the opposite sex. In September, Fenway can be slower if the team is out of contention, but is buzzing with excitement and filled to the brim with rabid fans if the Sox are battling for the divisional crown. Because of Fenway's allure and charm, its slowest moments are still characterized by a full house of fans.

Opponent

"Who are the Sox playing tonight?"— a common question asked by fans considering a game. Games against arch rivals (Yankees, Blue Jays) are more exciting and sought after than against other teams. It should be noted, however, that attending games against the once-hapless Cleveland Indians became quite fashionable for a while, with fans wearing Indians caps with the price tags dangling.

Pitching Match-Ups

Predicting a game's starting pitcher can be done at most a few days before the game. This can be accomplished if you know the team pitching rotation. For example, if the Red Sox starting rotation is (1) Clemens, (2) Viola, (3) Sele, (4) Darwin, and (5) Hesketh, and Sele pitched on Tuesday night, you can predict with reasonable certainty that Clemens will pitch on Friday night, three games after Sele. Star pitchers (such as Roger Clemens) are always worth going out of your way to watch if you appreciate good pitching. If you want to see lots of hits and runs, your best bet is to pick games with the worst pitchers. Most fans generally select a game without concern for the pitchers. The pitching match-ups just add to the flavor of the game.

Reading the Pitching Match-Ups in the Newspaper:
In the Boston Globe Sports Section (or any major newspaper sports page) look for a section entitled "Today's Probable Pitchers/Latest Line"

AMERICAN LEAGUE

			1992		Team	1992 vs. opp.			Last 3 starts			
		Time	Odds	W-L	ERA	Rec.	W-L	IP	ERA	W-L	IP	ERA	AHWG
BOS	Dopson (R)	2:05	8-9	6-4	3.39	6-5	0-0	0.0	0.00	2-1	18.0	3.50	14.5
At MIN	Krueger (L)			9-2	3.19	15-3	0-0	7.2	3.52	2-0	17.0	5.29	10.1
MIL	Bones (R)	2:35	6½-7½	5-5	4.95	9-7	0-1	2.0	18.00	1-2	14.0	10.29	20.6
At CHI	Hibbard (L)			7-4	4.20	10-8	0-1	6.2	6.75	1-0	18.0	4.00	13.5
CLE	Scudder (R)	2:35	7-8	6-8	4.94	6-11	0-1	6.2	1.35	1-2	12.2	8.53	20.6
At KC	Aquino (R)			0-1	12.27	0-0	0-0	0.0	0.00				
NY	Young (R)	4:05	5½-6½	1-2	5.04	0-1	0-0	0.0	0.00	1-1	13.1	7.43	18.9
At CAL	Blyleven (R)			3-3	5.21	3-6	0-0	6.0	4.50	0-2	9.0	16.00	24.0
DET	Ritz (R)	4:05	7½-8½	2-3	5.68	3-5	1-0	8.2	2.08	1-1	13.1	7.43	16.9
At OAK	Nelson (R)			1-1	6.63	0-1	0-0	7.0	3.86	0-0	3.1	5.40	21.6
TOR	Wells (L)		6-7	4-4	3.29	3-3	0-0	0.0	0.00	1-2	15.2	4.60	12.6
At SEA	DeLucia (R)	4:35		3-5	6.05	3-7	0-0	9.0	3.00	0-1	12.0	5.25	12.8
BAL	Rhodes (L)	8:05	7-8	1-0	2.35	1-0	0-0	0.0	0.00	1-0	7.2	2.35	9.4
At TEX	Burns (R)			2-2	3.49	2-5	0-0	1.2	10.80	0-1	21.1	2.95	7.6

NATIONAL LEAGUE

			1992		Team	1992 vs. opp.			Last 3 starts			
		Time	Odds	W-L	ERA	Rec.	W-L	IP	ERA	W-L	IP	ERA	AHWG
SD	Lefferts (L)	1:35	E-6	10-6	3.54	12-6	0-0	0.0	0.00	1-1	19.0	3.79	12.8
At MON	Gardner (R)			8-7	3.61	9-9	1-0	8.0	2.25	2-1	20.0	2.70	10.4
LA	Ojeda (L)	1:35	E-6	5-4	3.01	8-8	1-0	9.0	0.00	2-0	21.2	0.83	10.8
At PHI	Mk. Williams (R)			1-1	6.16	1-2	1-0	9.1	4.82	1-1	18.2	4.34	9.6
SF	Burkett (R)	1:40	6-7	6-5	4.07	11-7	0-1	1.1	13.50	1-1	20.0	3.60	9.5
At NY	Schourek (L)			1-3	2.85	2-6	0-0	0.0	0.00	1-0	20.2	2.61	8.3
St.L	M. Clark (R)	2:15	6½-7½	2-3	2.79	3-5	0-0	0.0	0.00	2-1	23.0	0.39	7.4
At CIN	Hammond (L)			5-5	3.71	10-5	0-0	0.0	0.00	0-2	17.2	4.08	12.2
ATL	Leibrandt (L)		6½-7½	7-3	3.64	11-5	0-0	0.0	0.00	1-1	16.1	4.41	12.1
At HOU	Henry (L)	2:35		3-6	4.58	8-10	0-0	0.0	0.00	1-0	17.2	2.55	13.2
CHI	Castillo (R)	8:05	8-9	6-7	3.21	7-10	0-0	0.0	0.00	1-1	20.2	3.05	9.1
At PIT	Smith (L)			8-7	2.96	12-7	0-0	0.0	0.00	3-0	23.1	0.39	6.2

KEY: Team rec. – Team's record in games started by today's pitcher. AHWG – Average hits and walks allowed per game in last 3 starts.

(usually found below the standings). Quite a bit of information can be found in this section, including the game times. Most games begin at 7:05 p.m. on weeknights, and 1:05 p.m. during the day.

Beginning with the left column, you can identify the teams playing one another (the first is the home team). Next to each team is the name of the pitcher starting the game. In parentheses next to each pitcher is R or L, indicating right or left-hander. The time of the game is shown next, along with the odds for those confident enough to bet on a baseball game. The next two columns show the pitchers' performance up to that point in the season. W-L indicates the pitchers' record (wins and losses), and ERA indicates their earned run averages. (ERA is basically the number of runs the pitcher is yielding on average, in a 9- inning game.) The rest of the columns provide information about the team's record when the pitcher starts the game, the pitcher's success (or failure) against the opponent this year, the pitcher's performance in his last three starts, and (for the number crunching geeks) — the average number of hits and walks the pitcher has yielded per 9 innings in his last three starts (AHWG).

Red Sox Promotions

The Red Sox offer special promotions throughout the year, focusing their attention to the younger fans and their families. (This means complimentary souvenirs!) Call the Red Sox Ticket Office at (617) 267–1700 for more details.

Ordering Tickets

Walk-up

Tickets can be purchased at either the Red Sox Ticket Office, (4 Yawkey Way at Fenway Park, open Monday through Saturday 10 a.m. – 5 p.m;

open until 7:05 p.m. before night games), or at the three Red Sox Clubhouse shops (located in Burlington Mall, Burlington MA; Emerald Square Mall, North Attleboro, MA; Northshore Mall, Peabody, MA). These locations do not accept phone orders. If you can get to either of these locations during the day, you will save yourself the grief of either waiting in long lines before the game to pick up your tickets, or anxiously waiting for them to arrive in the mall. Buying tickets in person also saves you the notorious $3 "handling charge" for your order.

It you're planning a last minute trip to Fenway on the day of the game, you have no choice but to buy your tickets at Fenway's ticket office up until game time. If you can't get there in time, you can still buy tickets from Gate A (see page 61).

Tickets By Phone

For ticket availability and to purchase tickets, phone the Direct Charge Line at (617) 267–1700. Master Card, Discover Card, and Visa are accepted. You will pay a $3 shipping and handling charge for the entire order, and if you are ordering 10 days in advance they will mail the tickets to you. Otherwise, you must pick up your tickets before the game at the Reservations Window next to Gate A (see page 61).

Tickets By Mail

If you want to order through the mail, specify the date of game(s), the quantity, and the price. Make your check or money order out to "Boston Red Sox." If you are using Master Card, Discover Card, or Visa, include the exact name printed on your card, the card number, and expiration date. Add $3 for shipping/handling for the entire order and include your return address and daytime phone number. Mail your order to Boston Red Sox Ticket Office, 4 Yawkey Way, Boston, MA 02215–3496.

Tickets By Fax

For those who are hopelessly hooked on fax machines, you can fax your request to the Ticket Office at (617) 236–6640. Include the same information required for mail orders as described above.

Discounted Ticket Program

During the course of a season, Fenway typically offers a variety of special games, such as family games (head of household pays full price, rest of family half price), Youth Group (15 or more) games (19 games, fans 15 years of age and younger admitted to bleachers for half price), Senior Citizen games (19 games, fans 65 and over can purchase reserved grandstand tickets for half price), and Red

Sox promotions (approximately 4 games, various souvenirs given out to fans).

Call the Red Sox Ticket Office at (617) 267–1700 to find out more about these special games.

Red Sox Ticket Exchange Policy

If you're in a situation where you can't use your tickets, you're in luck. Unlike Celtics, Bruins, and Patriots tickets, you can exchange Red Sox tickets for future games provided you make the exchange at least 1 week before the game. Exchanges are honored for non-season tickets only. Follow the instructions on the back of the tickets.

Guided Tours

Tours of Fenway are conducted Monday through Friday, May through September, at the following times: 10 a.m., 11 a.m., 12 p.m., and 1 p.m. Call Fenway Tour Information at (617) 236–6666.

Early Bird Tip!

For the diehard fan, tickets for the entire season officially go on sale the first Saturday of December. Expect a long line of fans formed down Yawkey Way for this traditional rite of passage. You can stand in line and extol the virtues of the Sox's latest free agent acquisition.

Finally, if you still have questions regarding tickets, try the Boston Red Sox Ticket Guide, a sixteen page reference which the Red Sox provide each season.

The Hazards of Buying From Scalpers

A trained eye can pick them out of the crowd. They're wearing athletic, bright colored clothes. They almost always have an obnoxious, impatient expression and a snake-like demeanor. It is inadvisable to buy tickets illegally through scalpers because of the following tactics:

1. Scalper sells you tickets with incorrect date.

2. Scalper sells you tickets which are not next to each other.

3. Scalper sells you lousy tickets in supposed "dream location."

4. Scalper does not allow you to reconsider once you are holding the tickets and he has your money.

Note: It is also **illegal** to re-sell a ticket (even at face-value) once it has been purchased.

Picking the Best
Place to Sit

Bleachers

$8 — Perhaps the most jovial section in Fenway, it is probably best suited for young, rowdy fans interested in harassing opposing pitchers in the bullpen. These seats are the farthest from home plate (and thus, farthest from the majority of the action), but fans enjoy the section for its fun-loving atmosphere and panoramic view of Fenway from its far corner. The bleachers are great on warm, summer days, but because there is no shade in this area be sure to bring sunscreen. If rain is a possibility, remember that you will be completely exposed to the elements.

Don't let the term "bleachers" fool you — all the seats have backs, as do all the seats at Fenway. **Section 34,** named the "Triangle" after its triangular shape, is the furthest section over in the bleachers towards center field, and allows you the opportunity to later say "I sat in the infamous triangle" (that's it, folks). The lowest rows of **sections 40 through 43** allow you to watch the pitchers warm up in the bullpens before and during the game. If you have no preference, you'll find that all the seats in the bleachers present a clear, unobstructed view of the field.

There are some drawbacks to sitting in the bleachers. Most seats in the bleachers do not have a clear view of the main scoreboard, as it resides in the back-center of the section. However, the auxiliary scoreboards showing ball, strikes, the score, etc. can be seen above the first and third base lines. You will be isolated from the rest of the park, so if you want to walk around and take in the many angles of Fenway you'll find the bleachers too confining.

Reserved Grandstand

$12 — The majority of the seats at Fenway are in the reserved grandstand section. **Sections 5 through 12,** along right field, can become quite uncomfortable because you'll have to strain your neck to the left to follow the action at home plate and the pitchers mound. After about 6 innings, you'll want to turn your head the other way to the right and stare at random people for a couple of innings. (Schedule an appointment with your chiropractor for the next day after the game if you plan to sit in these sections.) If you're not the type to closely monitor every pitch at the plate, you'll find that these sections offer a great view of the entire park. **Sections 1 through 4** are positioned at a more comfortable angle to see home plate, but you'll be almost as far away from home plate as the bleachers are. **Sections 1 and 2** are no smoking sections.

Sitting along the left field side is a much better prospect. **Sections 28 through 33** are angled more towards the playing field. The ideal section to sit in is **Section 30,** with its clear view of the entire playing field. **Sections 24 through 27, and 13 through 17** also contain prime seats, as you will be seated between home plate and either first or third bases. **Section 24** is another great location between third and home. **Section 33** should be singled out as a unique area to sit — you will be seated right down the left field line next to the Green Monster (see Chapter 3), and have a good shot at watching fair or foul balls fly by your very eyes. **Sections 32 and 33** are non-smoking and alcohol-free zones. **Sections 20 through 23** will seat you directly behind home plate. Many fans enjoy this view of the pitcher/hitter confrontation, but must watch it through a protective net.

If you're concerned about rain, be sure to request **rows UU through 16,** which are under Fenway's grandstand facade. Sitting in **rows 14 through 16** (the last 3 rows of the section), however,

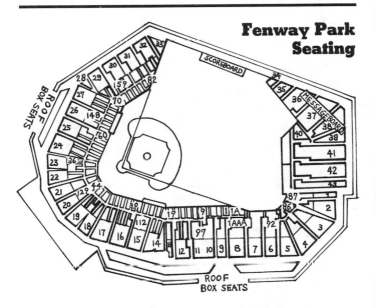

Fenway Park Seating

will place you close to the noisy traffic of fans walking to beer and hot-dog stands. In these last few rows you may also be near the "standing room only" area, which sometimes contains tired, impatient fans — many who are often loud and slightly inebriated.

Upper Box Seats

$16 — For the general public, the best attainable seats are in the upper box sections. These present great views of Fenway, close to the field, with **sections 112 through 148** seating you the closest to the infield. In contrast, **sections 21 through 43,** high above Fenway, are available for the same price.

Roof Box Seats

$16 — These seats place you high above the action, either on the third base side or the right field side of the diamond.

Field Box Seats

$20 — These seats are best for the baseball aficionado, but are available only to long-time season ticket holders. However, in the late innings don't be shy about sneaking down to these seats. You'll be awed by how close you have suddenly come to the playing field.

The 600 Club

These seats are generally reserved by corporations for business entertaining, and are located atop Fenway's original structure, high above home plate. It has been blamed for causing the wind to swirl around inside Fenway instead of traveling outwards (as it once did), and effectively reducing Red Sox players' home run totals since its construction.

Private Suites

Again, these seats are available only to season ticket holders who enjoy drinks, snacks, and television monitors along with the standard menu of Sox entertainment.

Standing-Room-Only Seats

$7 — Whenever a game is sold out, the standing-room-only area is opened in the corridor behind the reserved grandstand section, from home plate to right field. Your legs may get tired after several innings, but every die-hard should try this at least once! The Red Sox typically sell out over 50% of their games, so call the Red Sox Ticket Office beforehand to see if these tickets will be available.

Alcohol-Free Sections

No alcohol is allowed in Reserved Grandstand **sections 32 and 33** (first-come-first-serve availability).

Handicapped Seating and Access

Fenway has special rows for wheelchairs and handicapped entrances and seating access. The Red Sox have increased their handicapped seating to several sections. Call the Red Sox Main Office at (617) 267–8661 for details.

How to Drive to Fenway

From the Mass Pike

On Route 90 East (Mass Pike) take the Prudential Exit in Boston. Take a sharp right off the exit, and at the Sheraton Boston take a right onto Dalton Street. Turn left onto Boylston at the light. At the second set of lights, take a right onto Ipswich Street and follow to Fenway.

From Rhode Island

On I–95 North follow the Dedham/Maine/New Hampshire split. Take exit 20A/Route 9 East. Travel on Route 9 East for approximately 10–12 miles. Pass the Chestnut Reservoir, and at the sign for Kenmore Square on the left, take a left onto Brookline Avenue and follow it to Fenway.

From Cape Cod

Travel on Route 3 to the Boston split and continue northbound to Storrow Drive. Take Storrow to the Fenway/ Kenmore Square exit. At the top of the exit ramp, bear right onto Boylston Street, and take a right onto Yawkey Way after two sets of lights. Fenway is on the right.

From Coastal New Hampshire and Maine

Travel on I–95 South to Route 1 South towards Boston. Cross the Mystic Tobin Bridge, and at the split follow signs for Boston/Cape Cod. Where the road intersects Route 93 South, bear to the right and follow signs for Storrow Drive. Take Storrow to the Fenway/Kenmore Square exit. At the top of the exit ramp, bear right onto Boylston. Take a right onto Yawkey Way after two sets of lights. Fenway is on the right.

From New Hampshire
(Nashua, Hudson, Amherst)

Travel on Route 3 to Route 128 South to Route 2 Boston/ Cambridge. Follow Route 2 to the end and bear right at the lights. Pass through the next set of lights and over the bridge (Fresh Pond Mall is on the left). Take a left around the rotary and bear right at the next rotary (don't go around rotary). After three sets of lights, follow signs for Storrow Drive. Take Storrow to the Fenway/Kenmore Square exit. At the top of the exit ramp, bear right onto Boylston. Take a right onto Yawkey Way after two sets of lights. Fenway is on the right.

From Central New Hampshire and Vermont

Travel on Route 93 South to Boston. At the lower deck of bridge, bear right and follow signs for Storrow Drive. Take Storrow to the Fenway/ Kenmore Square exit. At the top of the exit ramp, bear right onto Boylston. Take a right onto Yawkey after two sets of lights. Fenway is on the right.

Traffic Tips

There are 5 major paths into Boston:

1. Mass Pike/Route 90 East
2. Expressway Northbound
3. Route 93 South
4. Tobin Bridge
5. Sumner Tunnel

All of these routes are heavy with traffic due to the large number of commuters leaving and entering the city after work and the asinine highway design. When afternoon traffic combines with game traffic, congestion can become even worse. The lower deck of the Central Artery, the Sumner Tunnel, the Tobin Bridge, and Storrow Drive are usually heavily filled with traffic both from commuters

 passing through the area and the Fenway crowd. **Avoid the central artery if at all possible.** On day-games, the Tobin Bridge,

the lower deck, and the expressway are not so bad because the commuters are gone. Also, try to avoid Route 9 (Boylston Ave.) because there are too many lights. The Mass Pike is the least congested and easiest route from the highway.

Your best bet is to listen to WBZ 1030 AM, which provides traffic updates every 10 minutes on the :03 minute. Before heading to the game, check the updates for major traffic jams or accidents.

Of these routes, the Mass Pike is by far the least likely to become congested. You will have to pay tolls, but it's worth the aggravation you'll spare yourself.

If you hate driving in traffic, you may want to consider taking the rapid transit line from Braintree, or parking farther away from Fenway and walking.

Parking Guide

P arking near Fenway can be irritating, time consuming, and a ripoff if you don't know what you're doing. For the educated fan, however, parking near Fenway can be a simple exercise.

Rating Key

★★★★ Fenway parking connoisseur's choice

★★★ Seasoned Boston sports fan's pick

★★ Only under extreme time duress

★ Watch out for the man with the slim-jim!

1. Masco Lot ★★★

Corner of Brookline and Yawkey. For $10 your car will be parked outside without being boxed in. You will see a sign "Red Sox Ticket Office across street," and the lot is located to the left of this sign, next to Boston Beer Works. This lot is often full.

2. Landsdowne Garage ★★★

Landsdowne Street across from park. The cost is $10, with most cars parked indoors, and none boxed in. This seems to be a good deal.

3. VIP Parking ★★★

Corner of Yawkey and Van Ness (and other adjacent lots). The cost is $10, almost all the cars are unblocked, and some are even parked inside a garage. This lot is staffed by several red-shirted, professional attendants. They will keep your keys during the game.

4. Leahy Mobil ★★

Corner of Boylston and Yawkey. For $12 your car will be parked with a chance of being boxed in.

5. Pilgrim Parking ★★

Corner of Yawkey and Van Ness. For $12 your car is boxed in.

6. LAZ Parking ★★

(Pronounced "lazy") Corner of Ipswich and Van Ness. For $12, your car will be boxed, but adequately protected. A lazy choice.

7. Texaco Parking ★

Corner of Boylston and Ipswich. You pay $15 to have your car boxed in while an attendant walks around with a slim jim for "emergencies."

8–9. Best Bets

8. Parking Away From the Park ★★★★

If you want to park farther away and walk or take MBTA (the subway) to the park, you will save yourself a great deal of grief from the nightly traffic jam around Fenway after the game. Park on Brookline Ave. or Beacon St. in the metered spots. This will leave you with an enjoyable 5–10 minute walk to the park.

9. The Prudential Center Garage ★★★★

The best bet is to park at the **Prudential Center Garage,** located on Boylston Street between Dartmouth and Exeter, and walk to the Park. Get there from the Mass Pike by taking the Prudential Center/Copley exit. You'll pay only $5 for parking if you present your ticket stub after the game. Your car will be parked indoors, unblocked, and you keep the keys. What's even better is that you can stay parked there from 5 p.m. to 1 am. To leave the lot after the game, simply turn off Boylston, take a left on Newbury, and you'll be back on the Mass. Pike in two blocks.

Fenway Fan's Parking Guide

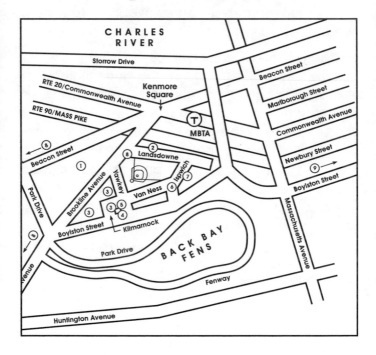

Alternatives to Driving

Walking to the Game

Most walking routes to Fenway through the city are enjoyable. If you have some extra time before the game, take a stroll through the Back Bay down Commonwealth Avenue or Newbury Street, towards Fenway. After crossing Mass. Ave, continue down Commonwealth or Beacon. You should avoid walking through the Back Bay Fens, a park located near Fenway (see map below). This area may seem inviting, but it is not safe to walk through, especially at night. When you reach Kenmore (via Commonwealth or Beacon), take a left onto Brookline.

Public Transportation

Taking the MBTA is a simple and cheap way of getting to and from Fenway If you don't want to walk or drive. Subways on the Green Line tend to get crowded before and after the game, so don't expect to sit. Fenway is located off the Green Line at the Kenmore Square stop. The fare is 85 cents (1 token).

If you are coming from the Braintree vicinity, take exit #17 (Washington/Union Street) off of Route 3, just off of Route 128. At this MBTA station (called Braintree), you can park your car for a mere $2.50 for the entire day. The ride to Boston takes approximately 25 minutes. Take the Red Line into Boston, switch to the Green Line at Park Street Station, and get off at the Kenmore stop. This puts you on Commonwealth Avenue — take a left on Brookline to walk to Fenway. The entire trip will cost 2 tokens ($1.70). When you leave Fenway simply follow the directions in reverse. The last train to Braintree leaves Boston at 12:30 am. For more information about other commuter rail routes, call the MBTA at (617) 722–5000.

SUBWAY LINES, COMMUTER RAIL AND BOAT

Ⓣ...The Alternate Route.

© MBTA 1993

MASSACHUSETTS BAY TRANSPORTATION AUTHORITY • WILLIAM F. WELD, GOVERNOR • ARGEO PAUL CELLUCCI, LT. GOVERNOR • JAMES J. KERASIOTES, SECRETARY OF TRANSPORTATION & MBTA CHAIRMAN • JOHN J. HALEY, JR. GENERAL MANAGER

Map courtesy of the MBTA ©

What to Bring

Observe the weather conditions, dress appropriately, and bring the necessary extras such as a wind-breaker for windy, colder weather, an umbrella in case of rain, and sunscreen on sunny days. Sporting white and red garments will reinforce your Red Sox loyalty, as will wearing a Red Sox hat or T-shirt. Since you will most likely be sitting in the "common-man" areas, don't wear expensive, silk garments, because spilled bear or mustard are facts of life at any ballpark. Small children and infants can be wrapped in swaddling Red-Sox colors. Sun glasses (and regular glasses) are a plus, as are opera glasses or binoculars. You are allowed to bring a camera, so if it's convenient bring it and capture Fenway's colorful charm. Be careful about bringing too many things, however, as there is very little room in front of and under your seat. One last thing...make sure to bring this book!

What Not to Bring

First, avoid wearing hats and/or paraphernalia from other baseball teams (especially the Yankees or Blue Jays). Harmless as it may seem, you risk being harassed by Red Sox fans in your section. There are several items which Red Sox security will not allow you to enter with: beach balls, inflatable dolls (yes, they have had problems with them in the bleachers), alcoholic beverages, beverages in glass bottles, and aluminum cans. If you're bringing a lunch, Fenway security may search your bags and ask you to leave cans and bottles behind.

How to Woo Your Woman into Letting You Go to the Game
(For Men Only)

Men, you all know how hard it can be to unshackle that ball and chain from your leg and get out to the Park. But that's the price you pay for love! Whether it's your girlfriend, fiancée, or wife, try these proven techniques which will produce measurable results for you:

PLAN A: Walk in the house/apartment and pretend that she's already agreed to go to the game. Stride in confidently, and while hurriedly changing your clothes, remark, "OK, honey, are you almost ready to go to the park?" This technique works most effectively if she has a poor memory.

PLAN B: If Plan A fails, imply that some commitment exists, one which would be difficult to get out of. "But honey, the Johnsons have already planned to go with us." Or, "Dear, I already bought the tickets over the phone!"

PLAN C: If Plans A and B have failed, it's time to really put on the charm. Try sweet cooing noises in her ear, followed by an innocent, "Please, can't we go to the game tonight?" in a baby-like quiver.

PLAN D: If Plan C doesn't work, you're going to have to make some sacrifices. Promise to take out the garbage, iron the shirts, wash the dishes, or any other chores that need to be done when you return from the game. (Don't worry, when you get back from the game, simply collapse in bed and feign a heavy sleep.)

PLAN E: If she won't go for Plan D, try relating to her a poignant childhood story of when your dad took you to your first game at Fenway, and allow your voice to "choke up" a bit. (Attempting this technique while dicing onions is most effective.)

PLAN F: Still no success? Try putting her on the defensive: "But honey, Frank Viola is pitching tonight!" (then add, under your breath, "I think...")

PLAN G: If she says, "No, Viola pitched last night!" then you will have to handle her exact objections face to face. If she complains that the game is just too boring, assault her with a flurry of rebuttals, such as citing the great weather, or the current Sox winning streak. Entice her with a delicious "dinner out" before the game. (It will be those great sausages outside Fenway!) You can also try, "Honey, we don't have to stay the whole game" (cross fingers behind back). If all else fails, try the line, "Don't you enjoy my company anymore?" with your head cocked at a pitiful angle with sad puppy eyes.

PLAN H: If nothing has worked up to now, you're in trouble. Drop to your knees, grab her legs and feet, and start begging. Don't let go until she gives in.

How to Leverage Your Position of Power With Your Man
(For Women Only)

So, your man is always harassing you about letting him go to sporting events. But shackling him in the house isn't the answer. You must use a two-pronged strategy:

1. Go to a game with him. If you're already a fan, treat yourself to a night out in the fresh air and enjoy just being togethor.

   If you're not yet a fan, go anyway! You will gradually learn to love baseball, and actually enjoy the outings. Plus, you can keep your eye on him this way. How do you become a baseball fan? Well, by reading this book cover to cover you'll know more about Fenway than he does. Start reading the sports section of the newspaper (in private, of course!), and various sports magazines such as Sports Illustrated. Also, watch the sports segment of the evening nows. If you're puttering around the house, listen to the Sox on the radio.

2. And now the more critical part: pretend you are not really that big of a sports fan, but are joining him because you love him so much! This allows you to leverage your power position — you are in the driver's seat now! The way to do this is through the magic of...

...THE POINT SYSTEM!!

Even if you are a fan, you can still pretend you're not up for it (headache, long day at work, weather, etc.). Every time you "do him a favor" by going to the game, assign a certain number of points to this favor (the two of you will agree on this number each time), and you'll find that it can become quite large when the Sox are playing the Yankees, or the weather outside is gorgeous. Now that you've agreed on the value of the favor, get it in writing. Have a written table of favors, with various point values associated with them. Whoever has fewer points owes the other various favors.

If the game is worth 3 points, for example, and he's in the red for three games (total of 9 points owed), think of all the great things he has to do for

you! With his passion for sports, you'll probably always be on the receiving end. And he won't resent you for these favors because, after all, it is you who is allowing him to go to the game!

Sample Point Sheet

Back rub ....2 points
Paint toe nails..................2 points
Do dishes ....1 point
Treat dinner out..............3 points
Flowers all week.............5 points
Girls night out ....4 points

CHAPTER THREE

PLAY BALL!

Pre-Game Activities

On radio station WRKO 680 AM, there is a pre-game show 30 minutes before the game, with players and the Red Sox manager and general manager interviewed nightly. Tailgate barbecuing is not that easy because you will most likely be parked in tightly with other cars and won't have room for a barbecue (save this for a Patriots game!). If you want to have a snack, a drink, or a meal before the game, here are some suggestions:

Eat in the Park

The absolute best pre-game activity is getting into the park early, munching on some Fenway Franks, and taking in batting practice. The food inside the park is decent, and reasonably priced. Besides, the true baseball fan eats ballpark food, not fancy restaurant cuisine!

Boston Beer Works

At the corner of Brookline and Yawkey, this new restaurant/bar offers appetizers such as nachos and half-back ribs, full meals ranging from beer-basted burgers to various pasta dishes, and several kinds of house brews. You can watch the game or other sporting events on monitors there.

Cask 'n Flagon

Located at the corner of Landsdowne and Brookline. Similar to Boston Beer Works, this establishment has been a Fenway pre-game watering hole for years. They offer a full compliment of appetizers, meals, and adult beverages, along with a big-screen TV, and various games (video, basketball, etc.).

Pizzeria Uno

Located at the Corner of Beacon Street and Brookline, actually 645 Beacon St., this Pizza Restaurant offers Chicago-style deep-dish pizzas and the usual standard appetizers and desserts. This restaurant becomes jam-packed before games, so you should get there several hours before the game to beat the crowd.

Pizza Pad

Located at 540 Commonwealth Ave., this shop offers an alternative to Fenway's mediocre, hard-to-find pizza. They sell big, Sicilian-style slices outside the shop before games. They also have wrap-to-go subs and grinders.

Cornwall's Bar/Pub

Located below ground level between the Army/Navy Store and Dunkin' Donuts at 510

Commonwealth Avenue (across from the Kenmore subway stop), this small but homey pub possesses a "Cheers-like" atmosphere. Season ticket holders often arrive before the game for beers, burgers, Cajun chicken, and the fish of the day.

Batters Box

Located at the Corner of Yawkey and Brookline, this Fenway tradition offers indoor and outdoor (snack bar window) service for pizza, hot-dogs, burgers, peanuts, and more. This place gets very crowded before games, and remains open until 3 am.

Outdoor Food Vendors

Two sausage vendors seem to have distinguished themselves among all the others for Italian sausage. The first, **The Sausage Connection,** is located at the corner of Brookline and Landsdowne. These sausages (priced at $4) are smothered in peppers and onions on a roll. **Sweet Italian Sausage,** located at the corner of Van Ness and Yawkey, is easily spotted because all the employees are wearing bright green T-shirts. This sausage, a close second to the Sausage Connection, offers similar 9-inch sausages for $4, and also offers steak or Cajun chicken sandwiches for $5.

Getting Into the Park

Whew, I thought we would have to call in the fire department, my team's so hot." – Casey Stengel, after his NY Mets snapped a 17-game losing streak.

You can enter the park up to an hour and a half before game time. If you want to get the chance to see the players take batting practice and shag fly balls in the outfield, this is an excellent opportunity to do so. Try to go early, or, at least, to be on time. There's nothing like the feeling of already being seated, watching the players take the field, and standing for the National Anthem. Try not to arrive late. (Los Angeles Dodger fans are know for arriving late and leaving early!)

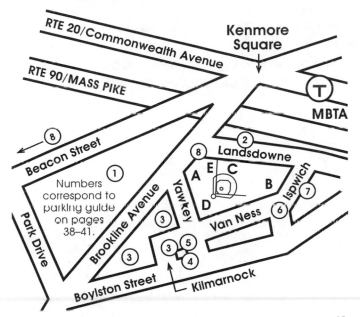

Finding your gate to enter Fenway can be a frustrating experience — many fans wander around the entire ballpark trying to find the right entrance. **Gate A** is the main gate, and the place to pick up prepaid tickets. For bleachers, enter through **Gate C** (located on Landsdowne St.). If you're sitting in right field, enter through **Gate B** (Ipswich Street), left field through **Gate E** (Brookline and Landsdowne), and anywhere in between the infield section through **Gate A** (Yawkey Way). **Gate D** is reserved for private suites and roof boxes.

Taking Care of the One You Love — Your Stomach

Find your seat first — then get your food. There is nothing worse than staggering through crowded sections of the park, arms full of teetering sodas and food, with your ticket in your mouth, trying to find your row ("excuse me, pardon me..."). It is also unpleasant for the other people you are rubbing elbows with.

There are roughly 20 concession stands throughout Fenway (5 located in the bleachers, 7 in right field, 2 in left field, and 2 behind home plate). There are several more on the upper and roof levels. Most stands offer hot dogs, sausage, popcorn, beer and soda. The exception is pizza, for which there are two stands in the entire park. These stands, called "Pizza Plus," sell cheese and pepperoni pizza by the slice or in whole form. If you want pizza, head directly behind **section 20** (behind home plate), or in the bleachers, and you will find "Pizza Plus" (with its traditional long line), and "Beer Express" next door.

If you're lazy and decide to wait for a vendor to come by with food, you may be waiting a long time for your dinner. Vendors only distribute hot dogs, soda, peanuts, and ice cream sports bars. You'll have to get up and seek out your beer, pizza, and other snacks.

Fenway Fan's Food Guide

Item	Price	Comments
Fenway Frank	$2.00	Still a classic with mustard
Polish Sausage	$3.00	1/4 pound polish kielbasa
Italian Sausage	$3.75	9" 5-1/2 oz. sweet peppers and onions on sesame roll
Chicken	$4.75	10 oz. breast, thigh, and drumstick with fries
Small Nachos	$2.50	Nachos with jalapeno cheese sauce and peppers
Large Nachos	$3.50	Nachos with jalapeno cheese sauce and peppers
Cheese Pizza	$1.75	Fresh made slices
French Fries	$1.25	9 oz. cup
Soft Pretzel	$1.75	6 oz. fresh pretzel with sesame seeds and salt
Popcorn Cup	$1.75	46 oz. cup with freshly made popcorn
Popcorn Bucket	$4.50	84 oz. souvenir bucket with handle
Crunch 'n Munch	$3.00	5 oz. box of buttery toffee with peanuts
Peanuts	$2.00	4 oz. bag — another classic

Fenway Fan's Food Guide (continued)

Item	Price	Comments
Yogurt Soft Serve	$2.50	5 oz. cone or cup with nonfat yogurt
Ice Cream	$1.75	"It's a Homer Bar" chocolate covered vanilla
Lemon Fantastic	$1.75	Lemon flavored dessert bar
Cookies	$1.00	3 chocolate chip cookies
Potato Chips	$.90	Local brand of fresh chips
Coffee	.90	8 oz. 100% Colombian fresh brewed
Soda	$1.50/$2.00	Coke, Diet Coke, Sprite, Nestea with lemon
Souvenir Soda	$2.50	Jumbo Souvenir Fenway cup
Evian Water	$2.00	Requested by fans several years ago
Beer	$3.25	Bud, Miller, Coors, in 14 oz. cups (bring your I.D.!)

Fenway Beer Rules

If you like to drink a few beers during a ball game, you should become familiar with "the beer rules." Study them, commit them to memory, for they shall govern your consumption at Fenway.

Rule 1: Thou Shalt buy only two beers at a time.

Rule 2: Thou Shalt not buy a beer without identification.

Rule 3: Thou Shalt leave your seat to seek out beer.

Rule 4: Thou Shalt not buy beer after the 7th inning.

Rule 5: Thou Shalt not drink beer in sections 32 and 33.

Rule 6: Thou Shalt not consume too much beer and be removed by security.

General Information

Telephones

Four phones are located on the lower level (with concession stands) under Reserved Grandstand **sections 32/33, sections 21/22, sections 23/24, and section 6.** In addition you will find a phone in the bleachers under **sections 36/37.**

Men's/Ladies' rooms

In the Reserved Grandstand area, men's rooms are located on the lower level (with concession stands) in left field, between home and 1st base, and in right field (two). Ladies' rooms can be found in left field, between home and third base, behind home plate, and in right field (three). The bleachers contain 1 men's and 1 ladies' room. There are several on the upper and roof levels (upper levels means behind last rows in Grandstand).

Customer Service Booths
Located behind home plate on lower level with concession stands, and under the bleachers.

Souvenir Stands
Various souvenir stands are located in left field behind home plate, and in right field. The Landsdowne Shop, located behind **section 30** in Reserved Grand-stand, has authentic and replica souvenirs.

Water Fountains
Scattered throughout the concession areas.

First Aid
Located under **section 13** in concession area.

Lost and Found
Finally, if you lose anything at Fenway report it immediately at the information booth. If you discover a missing item after you have left, call Fenway's "lost and found" number at (617) 267–9440.

Following the Game

During the course of the game you will discover several areas of the park which provide you with information on player statistics, the score of the game, the score of other games in progress, and the current number of strikes, balls, and outs.

There are two small auxiliary scoreboards along the left and right field grandstand facades. The example below shows these scoreboards during a game between NY and Boston. The scoreboard show runs (R), hits (H), errors (E), the current inning (Inn), the current hitter's number (AB), balls (B), strikes (S), and outs (O).

	R	H	E	INN	AB	B	S	O
NY	2	5	1					
BOS	5	9	0	7	42	3	1	0

The main scoreboard, located deep in center field behind the bleacher sections, shows player statistics, and sometimes replays spectacular catches or home runs. Announcements, along with the Bickford's Baseball Quiz, and the "Guess the Attendance" game, are shown on this main scoreboard. Most fans follow the game by the traditional, manually operated scoreboard located in left field, (see Left Field Scoreboard on page 76).

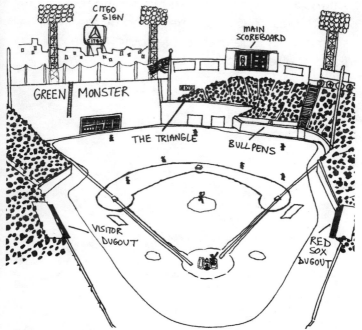

CITGO SIGN

MAIN SCOREBOARD

GREEN MONSTER

THE TRIANGLE

BULLPENS

VISITOR DUGOUT

RED SOX DUGOUT

Characteristics of Fenway

Dimensions

While every ballpark in baseball possesses its own unique dimensions, Fenway has by far the most interesting geometry. Home run hitters drool over the short distance from home plate down the left field line to the Green Monster, which reads a meager 315 feet. Fenway's dimensions are 302 to the right field foul pole, 380 down the right field line, a long 420 to deep center, 379 to the right of the Green monster in Left-Center Field, and an eye-opening 315 down the left field line to the foul pole.

The distance from home plate to the left field wall is controversial. Although "315 ft" is painted on the wall, almost everyone familiar with Fenway and the Red Sox disbelieves this number. In 1975 the Boston Globe used aerial photography to measure it at 304.779 feet. The Red Sox refuse to allow anyone to measure it, adding to the mystery.

The crowd is close to the field at Fenway, creating an intimacy not found in other ballparks and the smallest foul territory in the league. Fenway's nooks and crannies in left, center, and right, the triangular nature of the bleachers, and its majestic left field wall (called the Green Monster) make it totally unique to other sporting arenas. It is, simply put, the gem of baseball parks.

The Green Monster

(Also known as "The Wall.") Fenway's most famous attraction, the Green Monster, is known for its close proximity to home plate, its height, and its built-in scoreboard. Its presence can be a double-edged sword for hitters and pitchers alike. Routine fly balls become home runs if the wind is blowing out (watch the flag in center field for gusts of wind). Its towering height of 37 feet transforms high, lazy fly balls into cheap extra-base hits as the ball scrapes

off its surface on the way down. The Wall, however, can cut down heat-seeking, missile-like home run shots that are hit too low, turning them into doubles or even singles. Balls hit off the wall are called "wall-balls." Sometimes, balls are hit right at the scoreboard and bounce off at odd, unpredictable angles. This presents a nightmarish experience for the left fielder.

The Green Monster did not always look the way it does today. In 1947, The Wall was mostly covered with picture ads. The net above The Wall was installed in 1936 to protect windows on Landsdowne St. from home run balls. Before it was resurfaced with hard plastic in 1976, The Wall consisted of wooden railroad ties, covered with tin. Balls hit off the tin portion of The Wall would drop straight to the ground with a thud. The Green Monster possesses the league's only "in-play" ladder, which starts 13-1/2 feet above the ground and rises along the left corner of The Wall. It is used by groundskeepers to retrieve balls hit into the net during batting practice before the game.

Left Field Scoreboard

You will find the grand daddy of all scoreboards in left field, located on the Green Monster. It is one of only two remaining manually-operated scoreboards in baseball. (Wrigley Field in Chicago has the other.) This scoreboard shows inning-by-inning totals of each team's runs, and keeps totals of hits, runs, and errors. Watch for the numbers to change when a run is scored. Each number is 16" x 16", weighs 3 lbs., and is changed manually by Fenway personnel. If you look closely, you will see a faint outline of a door leading behind the wall. Before the game Fenway personnel can be seen walking in and out through this door.

			A M E R I C A N		L E A G U E			
P		1 2 3 4 5 6 7 8 9 10	R H E	P	IN R	P		IN R
37	K.C.	0 0 0 3 0 0	3 5 0	36 NY	2	36 NY		2
49	BOSTON	2 0 1 0 0	3 5 0	35 CLEV	3 1	35 CLEV	3	1
				46 BALT	1	46 BALT		1
AT BAT	BALL STRIKE OUT Ⓗ	Ⓔ		37 TOR	2 1	37 TOR	2	1
24	●●● ●● ●● ●	●		49 DET		49 DET		
				40 CHI		40 CHI		

The scoreboard's charm comes in part from the traditional green and red bulb lights which indicate balls, strikes, and outs (red for strikes and outs, and green for balls). The "out of town" portion appraises you of the scores of all games being played that day in the American League. You may wonder what the two-digit number next to each team means. It represents the uniform number of the pitcher currently in the game for each team. Finally, the initials of the late Red Sox owners, Thomas A. Yawkey (TAY) and Jean R. Yawkey (JRY) appear in Morse code in two vertical stripes.

CITGO Sign

Built in 1965 atop a building on 660 Beacon St. in neighboring Kenmore Square, this Fenway mainstay looms over the Green Monster.

Jimmy Fund Sign

Located in right field above the grandstand, this fund has raised millions of dollars for the Dana Farber Cancer Institute in its fight against cancer in children.

Right Field

Fenway's right field is considered the most problematic in baseball, due to the close proximity of the bullpens to home plate and the odd angles the fielder must deal with if a ball is hit in the corner. This area is formed by the low railing and wall which curve out sharply from the pole into deep right field. Many cheap home runs have occurred as weak 302-foot pop-ups sail just past the foul pole into the stands.

Pesky's Pole

The right field foul pole was nicknamed "Pesky's Pole" by a sportswriter after former Red Sox player Johnny Pesky hit the pole for a game-winning home run.

Visitor and Home Bullpens

In 1940, the Red Sox, in part to help Ted Williams hit home runs, added the bullpens in right field. This addition, nicknamed "Williamsburg," reduced the distance from home plate by 23 feet. These "pens" are the place where the bullpen pitchers eat sunflower seeds, spit tobacco, play pranks on one another, warm-up, and watch the game until the bullpen phone rings. (Yes, the manager actually picks up a phone and calls the bullpen when he wants a pitcher to begin warming up.) Pitchers warming up in the pen quickly become subjected to crowd praise or abuse. When called upon, they enter the playing field through the bullpen doors, and trot across the outfield to the pitcher's mound.

Retired Numbers

Located on the green facade atop Fenway's right field grandstand, you will see four red numbers on white, circular backgrounds. These are the

numbers of the four Red Sox players whose numbers have been retired due to the following criteria: the players were inducted into the Baseball Hall of Fame, played at least 10 years with the Red Sox, and ended their careers with the Red Sox. The numbers read 9 for Ted Williams, 4 for Joe Cronin, 1 for Bobby Doerr, and 8 for Carl Yastrzemski.

These numbers, quite coincidentally, have come to symbolize 74 years of futility in attaining a World Championship, often termed "The Curse of the Bambino," in reference to the Red Sox sale of

Babe "the bambino" Ruth to the Yankees. The numbers, reading 9-4-1-8, match with September 4, 1918, the eve of the 1918 World Series. Babe Ruth would pitch the next day, win the first game of the series 1–0, and lead the Red Sox to their last World Series victory. A year later Red Sox owner Harry Frazee, financially strapped with the team and his theater business, would strike up a deal in which he would sell Babe Ruth to the Yankees for $100,000 in cash and a $300,000 loan in the form of a mortgage on Fenway Park. Since then, the Yankees have won 22 World Championships, the Red Sox — 0. Sweet move, Harry.

The 600 Club

This structure, which resides high above home plate, was added to Fenway in 1988, and consists of luxury boxes for the corporate crowd. Many have speculated that it has altered wind currents which originally traveled across the field and over the Green Monster. It has been blamed for a reduction in home runs hit by the Red Sox since the addition was made. Students at MIT have conducted numerous studies which seem to support this theory, and plan to propose, design, and test a wind-altering device which would redirect wind back over the wall.

Famous Spots

B esides being a baseball heaven, Fenway also serves as a virtual museum of Red Sox history. Here are a few slices of Fenway's past.

Foul Pole in Left Field

Carlton Fisk's famous 12th inning home run on October 22, 1975 in the World Series against Cincinnati stands as one of baseball's finest moments. Fisk's hooking drive bounced off the foul pole as he ran down the first base line, contorting

his body, willing the ball to stay fair. At 12:33 a.m., all of New England rejoiced in the knowledge that the Red Sox had forced a 7th and deciding game, and an opportunity for their first World Series victory since 1918.

Right Field in Front of Bullpens

Dwight Evans' famous catch in right field (in the same game) robbed the Reds' Joe Morgan of extra bases or even a home run, which would have lost the game and the Series for the Red Sox. Evans caught the ball on the run over his shoulder, turned, and fired to first base, picking the runner off for an inning-ending, game saving double play.

Bleachers

Only six balls have ever been hit out of the park to the right of the flag pole in centerfield. These hitters were: Hank Greenberg and Jimmy Foxx in 1937, Bill

Skowrun in 1957, Carl Yastrzemski in 1970, and Bobby Mitchell and Jim Rice in 1976.

Pitcher's Mound

In 1986, up-and-coming pitcher Roger Clemens, in the fourth game of his first full season with the Red Sox, shocked the baseball world by striking out a record 20 Seattle Mariners batters, breaking the record of 19 shared by Steve Carlton, Nolan Ryan, and Tom Seaver. The Sox won the game 4–1 and went on to win the American League Pennant.

Home Plate

During the final home game of the 1960 season, Red Sox great Ted Williams stepped to the plate in the 8th inning for the last time in his long career. The "Splendid Splinter" drove the last pitch he saw into the right field bullpen, and the crowd paid tribute with a thundering ovation as he rounded the bases one more time.

Fenway Favorites

Fenway Sights

- Walking from the far corner of left field (next to the Green Monster) to the far corner of right field (next to Pesky's pole), along the pathway in the lower grandstand area. When you start out, take a good look at the Green Monster and its intimidating presence. Take in the various vantage points of the game as you work your way to right field.

- Participating in the "Fenwave," which usually starts in the triangle in the bleachers, and almost always travels clockwise through the bleachers, into right field, and on through to left field.

- Watching the manager and the umpire arguing, escalating to the point where both are less than an inch apart, spraying saliva on each others faces, and always yelling at the same time.

- Watching the cleaning crew primp and preen the infield dirt and mound between the 5th and 6th innings.

- Watching beach balls ricochet around the bleachers, or even better, being in the bleachers and striking one of the balls.

- "Wall-ball," a game played frequently at Fenway, where the batter hits the ball at the Green Monster. The ball ricochets off the wall or scoreboard at weird, unpredictable angles, causing the unfamiliar, panic-stricken, visiting outfielder to scramble after the elusive ball.

- Watching the red and green lights on the Green Monster scoreboard whenever a strike, ball, or out is recorded.

- The grounds crew, under the tyrannical, militant leadership of Joe Mooney, covering the field during a rain delay.

- Witnessing the crowd's and players' reaction to a squirrel or a rat racing across the outfield.

- Watching a run changed manually on the left field scoreboard, and watching a score change on the "out-of-town" scoreboard during a pennant race as a rival team is embroiled in a close game in the late innings.

Fenway Sounds and Smells

- The home plate umpire howling or grunting a called third strike on a bewildered batter.

- The crescendo of the crowd cheering as a well struck ball rises majestically over the Green Monster and into the night for a home run.

- The National Anthem, and "Take Me Out to the Ball game," sung during the 7th inning stretch.

- The combination of mustard, hotdogs, fresh air, cigar smoke, bubblegum, and roasted peanuts: a unique scent only found in baseball parks.

- The smell of the leather of a baseball glove that you've brought to track down foul balls.

- The smell of sizzling sausages outside of Fenway Park at the vendor carts.

Talk Like a Fan

"Whenever I decided to release a guy, I always had his room searched first for a gun. You couldn't take any chances with some of those birds." – Casey Stengel

I f you really want to be part of the "Fenway faithful," you need to master the slang, the delivery, the attitude of a true Red Sox fan. The basic idea is to be wildly biased towards the Sox, wildly opposed to the other team, and fickle with the umpires. Booing should be reserved for members of the other team, and only under extreme conditions is it acceptable to lay your wrath on a Red Sox player. (Extreme condition example: The Red Sox clean-up hitter has not hit a home run in 2 months, is hitting below .200, has stranded 6 runners in the game thus far, and has just struck out with the bases loaded with the Red Sox down by 2 runs.)

Slang

Mastering Fenway fanhood also involves the use of baseball slang. Mastering the Boston accent can take years of practice, and is almost impossible to imitate properly by the novice. Your correct usage of words and expressions, however, will allow you to feel at home with the established "Fenway Faithful" in your section.

Sure-fire Expressions

The use of short, colorful expressions is common among Fenway fans. They are used primarily to summarize or observe situations on the field. They are often filled with emotions such as awe, sarcasm, wonder, cynicism, panic, or anger. Here are a few examples:

When the hitter strikes out:

- Say to the person sitting next to you, "He whiffed!!" or "He was blown away!"

- Yell at the player as he walks back to the dugout, "See ya!" or "Sit down!" or "Back to the minors!"

When the opposing pitcher is pitching poorly:

- Say to the person sitting next to you, "He's being lit up!" or "He's being shelled/shellacked/knocked around!"

- Yell to the pitcher after a big hit, "Nice pitch, Stottlemyre!" or "Give him another cookie, Stottlemyre!"

- Also, signal to the bullpen by touching outstretched arm (like manager does when he requests a pitching change).

When a Red Sox pitcher is wild:

- Say to the person sitting next to you, "He's all over the place!" or "He's got control problems!" or "He can't find the plate!"

- Yell to the pitcher as the count goes to 3 balls, no strikes, "Throw Strikes!"

When the opposing pitcher is removed from the game after a poor performance:

- Yell, "Sayonara!" or "Hit the showers," or "Back to the minors!"

- Sing along with organ, "Nah, Nah, Nah, Nah... Nah, Nah, Nah, Nah.... Hey, Hey, Hey... Goodbye!" (Raise beer while singing.)

   Practice these phrases and study the slang guide on the next three pages.

Guide to Fenway Slang

Slang	What it Means	Secondary Meaning
Aspirin tablet	fastball	cure for hangover
Baltimore chop	weak hit chopped off front of plate	imitation of Atlanta fans
Banjo Hitter	poor contact, makes sick sound	musician at bat
Batting practice pitch	weak, easy-to-hit fastball	pitch thrown during practice
Beanball	pitch which hits the batter	eatable pitch
Boot	fielding error	for illegally-parked car
Bridge Master	pitcher who allows too many homeruns	card-game genius
Brush back	pitch intentionally thrown close to batter	a useful shower tool
Bum	lousy player (used liberally for pitchers)	a person's underside
Bush league	lacking class (minor leaguer)	league for ex-presidents
Cheese	fastball	eatable mold
Chump	bum — used primarily for hitters	cousin of the chimpanzee
Comebacker	ball hit back at pitcher	boxer who keeps getting up
Cookie	an easy to hit pitch (see BP pitch)	a cute name for significant other
Cup of coffee	brief stint in majors with a team	morning drug
Dinger	homerun	hitting head on car door
Ducks on the pond	runners on base to be driven in	Boston Common sight
Duster	brushback	household tool

Eephus pitch	10-12 feet in air, blooper pitch	no secondary meaning
Flake	eccentric player (pitcher)	dandruff
Gas	good fastball	result of a Fenway hot-dog
Green light	freedom to swing	signals chaos in Boston traffic
Hanging curve	curve that doesn't break /easy to hit	popular female anatomy for men
Head-hunting	throwing at batters' heads	the pigeons above
Hill	mound	Anita's last name
Homer	homerun	Simpsons character
Hook	curve	Popular Peter Pan movie
Hot corner	3rd base	street corner in red-light district
Long-ball	also a homerun	book by Longfellow
Meatball	easy-to-hit pitch	Italian delicacy
Mop-up	pitch in relief way behind	janitor's duty
No-no	a no-hitter	words used by girlfriend
Ohfer	hitless day	grunting noise indicating pain
Out pitch	pitch pitcher depends on to get batter out	no secondary meaning
Payoff pitch	full count pitch	illegally-funded pitch
Punch and Judy hitter	well placed soft singles	puppet who can hit
Purpose pitch	pitch thrown at batter to intimidate	politically-correct pitch
Quail shot (dying quail)	weak hit dropping in front of outfielders	Murphy Brown's comments
Scroogie	screwball pitch	Ebeneezer's nickname

Sitting duck	runner is picked off , thrown out easily	ugly duckling's lazy brother
Southpaw	left-handed pitcher	left-handed dog
Spitball	doctored (Vaseline pitch, pine tar ball)	seen flying off Eifel Tower
Stiff	lousy player (used mostly for batters)	your lower back in bleachers
Tater	homerun	An American dinner treat
Texas league single	lofted weakly into shallow outfield	no secondary meaning
Twin killing	double play	bizarre murder case
Uncle Charlie	curve ball	your father's brother
Wounded duck	weakly hit pop-up	hunter's nightmare
Yakker	sharp breaking curve	a good joke
Yellow yammer	curve	yellow bird

Opposing Managers

If you are really getting into Fenway fanhood you probably will dislike the opposing team's manager. Managers come in all different shapes, sizes, and personalities. Here are some basic categories that the other team's manager will likely fall into:

Ex-Player

- Fiery, wishes he could pick up a bat and take a swing.
- Prone to throwing Gatorade jugs onto the field in anger.
- Often yells at and kicks dirt onto the umpire.

Gambler

- Manages on gut feeling, "rolls the dice" frequently.
- Goes against conventional wisdom.

Computer Man

- Too analytical.
- Has all kinds of charts and numbers.

Text book Manager

- Too theoretical.
- Manages from the old book.

Sleeping Beauty

- Sleeps in the dugout.
- Wakes up to call the bullpen, or to make the long walk to the mound (sleep walking?)
- Usually over the age of 55.

Captain Hook

- Removes starting pitchers too early.
- Shows no patience with them.

Dealing with Umpires

"Many fans look upon an umpire as a necessary evil to the luxury of baseball, like the odor that follows an automobile." – Christy Mathewson

Cardinal rule: Take any call against the Sox as a personal affront to your intelligence and integrity. Your goal is to sway the umpire's allegiance to that of the Red Sox.

Common Tactics Used with Umpires

- On a call against the home team, yell "Get some glasses!" or "Get your prescription changed!"

- Cheer on the Red Sox manager as he argues with the umpire.

- If the other manager argues, yell, "Kick him out, ump!"

- On close pitches called against the Sox, groan or boo the ump.

- If the opposing catcher goes to the mound to confer with his pitcher, groan, boo and yell at the ump to break it up.

Doing the Fenwave

1. Cheer it on to encourage it at beginning.

2. Make sure to stand up, throw hands and arms up, and yell loud incoherent things.

3. The wave should only travel from left to right field and around clockwise.

4. Don't start the wave too early in the game — wait until slow moments in the middle innings.

Special Rules for Dealing with Pitchers

- If the Red Sox relief pitcher is one strike away from ending the game, stand and clap rhythmically with the crowd in anticipation of the last out.

- When a Red Sox relief pitcher comes out of the bullpen to finish the game, bow and pay homage to encourage him if you are in bleachers near the bullpen. You can yell words of encouragement while he is warming up. For pitchers in the opposing team's bullpen, harass them and try to destroy their confidence. Relief pitchers are usually a wreck mentally because they have to come into pressure-packed

situations. They will always pretend they are cool and mean, but inside they're all frazzled. So let 'em have it!

• If a pitcher has a no-hitter (has not allowed any hits in the game), under no circumstances do you say the word "no-hitter" or directly acknowledge that the pitcher is doing this. It is bad luck, and will surely destroy the pitcher's karma.

CHAPTER FOUR

POST- GAME TIPS

If you're not too tired after the game and are looking for some fun and food to occupy yourself while traffic dies down, here are some post-game suggestions:

Souvenirs

The Souvenir Store — Twins Enterprises

Located on Yawkey Way across from Fenway, this vast souvenir store is the area's best for buying hats, T-shirts, posters, and other sports memorabilia. For small children (and some child-like adults), there is a baseball-shaped cart parked in the middle of the store. (Once upon a time it was used at Fenway to transport pitchers from the bullpen to the mound.) Your child may want to sit in it, and in return you are asked to make a small donation to the Jimmy Fund (Dana Farber Cancer Institute). Among the vast quantities of souvenirs, you will find yourself staring at old, quaint photographs of ballplayers from the past. This store is a must for the serious baseball fan, especially if you want a special souvenir from your Fenway experience.

Bowling/Billiards

RFA Amusements
(Formerly Kenmore Bowlradome.) Located under Fenway at the corner of Brookline and Landsdowne, this establishment offers 20 lanes of candlepin bowling, video games, and a pool room. Unfortunately, they close early at 10 p.m.

Jillian's Billiards
Located at the corner of Ipswich and Landsdowne. This establishment contains 40–50 pool tables, a whiffle ball batting cage, a basketball shoot-out game, pinball machines, video games, a table shuffle board, darts, and foosball, along with two bars and sitting areas. You will not be admitted if you're wearing sweat pants, tank tops, ripped jeans, or hats.

Night Clubs/Bars

Avalon, Axis, and Venus
Located along Landsdowne Street, these dance clubs attract patrons clad in dark clothes. If you're wearing chinos with white sneakers, you probably won't be admitted. Venus DeMilo features women dancing in cages (fully clothed, of course).

Cask'n Flagon, Boston Beer Works
Good for beer or food. See Chapter 2, page 57.

Shopping

Tower Records
Located on the corner of Newbury St. and Mass Ave, you'll find three floors of CD's, tapes, and records. With your Red Sox ticket stub you'll receive a $2 discount on most CD's or cassettes over $9.44. This discount also applies at their Cambridge store.

Leaving

If you're in traffic, turn to WRKO 680 am for the post-game show starring Joe Castiglione.

Extricating yourself and your car from the surrounding mess is largely dependent on where you parked. If you parked in large, congested lots near Fenway, you will have to endure leaving the lot, traveling along the narrow, winding, one-way streets of Boston, and finally, the traffic on the major highways. If you are one of many New Englanders who suffers from "traffic-phobia," (symptoms include, among other things: mood fluctuations, thrashing, claustrophobia, yelling, displaying profanity, itchiness, sweating), you may want to occupy yourself with some of the surrounding activities for about a half an hour before heading out. If you were smart enough to park away from Fenway, you will enjoy a pleasant walk back

 to your car, and an easier time leaving Boston.

CHAPTER FIVE

LIFE BEYOND FENWAY

(YES, IT DOES EXIST)

Alternatives to the Park:
TV and Radio Coverage

When you're not at Fenway you can still follow the Sox on TV for those important 3-game series against arch rivals. Catch the Sox game either on NESN (New England Sports Network) or on WSBK TV38. Check your local TV listings for the correct station.

Another option is to listen to the game on the radio. There's something pure about imagining the play while an announcer paints a picture for you. Plus, you can listen while you're doing other stuff—it's great background music. It's tough to remain on the edge of your seat for three hours if you're not at the park. That's why TV or radio work so well while you're working on other things.

Top 10 things to do while watching or listening to the Red Sox game:

10. Shining shoes

9. Ironing shirts/laundry

8. Cleaning/dusting room

7. Yard work

6. Lunch time on Saturday while wolfing down sandwich

5. Kissing / cuddling on couch at night

4. Barbequing

3. Drinking some beers in a sports bar

2. Sunbathing on the beach

....and the most popular activity to do while listening to /watching the Red Sox is.....

1. Slowly drifting off to sleep in bed.

PawSox!

Another great alternative to Fenway is a trip to the Red Sox AAA International Baseball League affiliate, the Pawtucket Red Sox (or PawSox). The PawSox play in Pawtucket, RI, at McCoy Stadium, a small but wonderful place where you will escape all the hustle, bustle, and big-time atmosphere of major league parks. Your seat is always close to the field — capacity is only 7,002. McCoy is a place where kids still seem like the important fans.

McCoy Stadium is famous for the longest game in baseball history, a 33 inning affair which occurred in 1981. The PawSox defeated the Rochester Orioles 3–2. They sell souvenir cups showing the scoring in all 33 innings.

Watching the PawSox at McCoy Stadium is great because it's easy to get there. From Northern points, just follow 95 South into Rhode Island and take exit 2A/Newport Avenue. Following the signs to McCoy, go 2 miles and take a right onto Columbus Ave. The stadium is located on Columbus Ave. If you're coming from the south, take 95N to exit 28/School Street. Bear right at the end of the exit. After two lights, take a left onto Pond Street and you'll spot the stadium.

Ticket prices are cheap — only $5.50 for box seats and $4.00 general admission. Tickets may be purchased in person at McCoy, by mail, or through Ticketmaster. For more information, call the PawSox at (401) 724-7300.

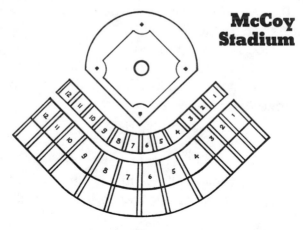

McCoy Stadium

Following the Sox on the Road

For those of you who do a lot of traveling, you sure know the agonizing feeling of not being able to follow the Sox, especially during a pennant race. Here are some suggestions for keeping up with the team:

1. Read the sports section in USA Today. It has the best sports coverage for the traveler, and you can usually find this newspaper anywhere, even overseas. (Warning: a USA Today newspaper, three days old, can sell for as much as 30,000 Yen, or about $30, at a hotel gift shop in Japan!]

2. ESPN does good work each night showing highlights of the day's ball games. They also broadcast games several nights during the week. Even if you happen to be traveling in California, there

are actually plenty of Red Sox fans on the West Coast. Thus ESPN often airs the Red Sox games there for those fans.

3. Try going to a baseball game in the city you're visiting. At least you'll be at the park, and all the stadiums show updated scores of all the games around the league so you can monitor the Sox throughout the game. Sampling different parks and stadiums is a lot of fun, and makes you appreciate Fenway's unique qualities.

CHAPTER SIX

FANHOOD QUIZ

Multiple Choice Test

1. Duffy's Cliff was named after:

    a. Duffy Lewis' beer-belly

    b. 10 ft. high cliff in front of the left field wall

    c. pile of stinky clothes in Duffy Lewis' locker.

    d. cliff in front of dugout

    e. none of the above

2. If you're planning a last minute trip to Fenway the day of the game, you should first try to:

    a. buy the tickets just before the game at the ticket office

    b. show up at Gate A and tell security that your dog ate your tickets

    c. dress up in your Red Sox uniform jersey and go through the players entrance

    d. give up

    e. look for scalpers

3. If you must buy scalped tickets, you should:

a. attach a sign to your chest reading "Need to buy illegal tickets"

b. ask a police officer where you buy the tickets from scalpers

c. stand around and look for the slick-looking people murmuring "tickets, tickets.."

d turn hat inside-out

e. none of the above

4. One disadvantage of sitting in the bleachers is that:

a. it's just too much goddarned fun!

b you sit on uncomfortable steel benches

c. you can't walk behind home plate

d. you can't order beer

e. none of the above

5. If you want to drink beers during the game, avoid:

   a. the old lady with the cane

   b. running on the field, beer in hand, with your pants down

   c. spilling beer on security guard's head

   d. section 33

   e. all of the above

6. If you're late for the game, your best bet for parking is to:

   a. abandon the car on Landsdowne St., turn your hazard lights on, lift the hood, and run to Gate A

   b. park in the Red Sox parking lot for $10

   c. drive directly into the park and out onto the field (disguise your car as a bullpen cart)

   d. double park on Ipswich Street since they never ticket cars there at night

   e. none of the above will work

7. The Red Sox will not allow you to bring which of these items:

    a. can of Sprite

    b. beach ball

    c. inflatable doll

    d. automatic weapon

    e. all of the above

8. You can't buy beer if you:

    a. don't have an ID

    b. wait until after the 7th inning

    c. stink like a drunk and vomit on the counter

    d. belch loudly into the attendant's ear

    e. all of the above

9. The real dimensions to the left field wall from home plate are:

    a. A mystery even to Babe Ruth's ghost

    b. 307 ft

    c. 312 ft

d. 315 ft

e. 35 smoots

10. Pesky's Pole was named after:

a. Johnny Pesky's favorite pool cue

b. infamous prank by teammates who hung Johnny Pesky's boxer shorts on the flag pole

c. foul pole off which Pesky hit game-winning home run

d. the bat with which Pesky hit three home runs in the 1946 World Series

e. none of the above

11. A pitcher throws a 95 mph fastball close to the batter's face. This is called:

a. a scroogie

b. a purpose pitch

c. a cookie

d. an ohfer

e. any of the above

12. When a pitcher is pitching a no-hitter, you must:

a. call the local papers at the pay phone behind home plate

b. chant, "no hitter, no hitter!"

c. get on your hands and knees and pray for divine assistance

d. say nothing

e. none of the above

13. If the umpire ejects the Red Sox manager from the game, you should:

a. cheer the manager

b. insult the umpire (and various family members)

c. elevate the manager to hero status

d. boo every subsequent call by the umpire

e. all of the above

ANSWERS

1. b	7. e
2. a	8. e
3. c	9. d
4. c	10. c
5. d	11. b
6. b	12. d
	13. e

SCORING

0–3 correct	Lost Yankee Fan
4–7 correct	"Standing-room-only" peon
8–10 correct	Bleacher bum
11–13 correct	Fenway Connoisseur

Fenway Puzzle

Find the 16 hidden words.

```
P  T  L  S  H  S  Q  A  Q  L  O  K  R
E  A  X  W  C  O  O  B  D  T  G  S  K
S  K  Y  B  O  X  R  U  S  P  J  T  B
K  A  W  L  G  P  P  L  X  C  S  R  L
Y  Y  B  E  C  K  F  L  F  I  E  R  E
S  C  R  A  U  B  Z  P  W  T  H  K  J
P  K  L  C  T  O  B  E  S  G  J  E  N
O  J  S  H  E  V  P  N  Y  O  T  A  A
L  N  I  E  W  A  O  K  N  S  O  W  H
E  T  M  R  J  M  G  S  K  I  H  S  P
B  F  I  K  N  O  R  D  U  G  O  U  T
R  C  S  E  C  U  I  I  J  N  M  B  A
U  U  E  G  K  N  C  N  T  S  E  D  T
W  R  K  B  G  D  M  G  H  Z  R  G  E
G  V  L  E  Z  J  L  C  R  A  S  O  R
L  E  R  O  S  R  B  R  X  L  C  B  N
```

Note: Waldo cannot be found in this puzzle.

ANSWER

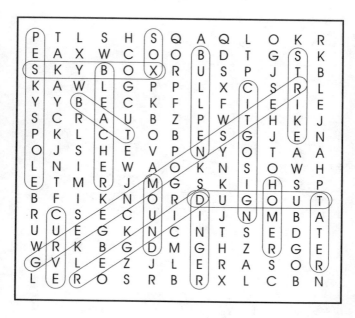